The Name of My Country

Also by Tunui John-Ngariki

Once Were Cannibals

The Name of My Country

Poems

by

Tunui John-Ngariki

Published by Tunui John-Ngariki
2016

Copyright Tunui John-Ngariki 2016
All rights reserved

John-Ngariki, Tunui   1962 –

The Name of My Country / poetry / Tunui John-Ngariki

ISBN   978-0-473-34794-9

Softcover   01/2016
I. Title

Print on Demand in the United States of America, Australia, France and the United Kingdom by Lulu Press (lulu.com)

This book is sold subject to the condition that it shall not, by way of trade or otherwise, be lent, resold, hired out or otherwise circulated without the publisher's prior consent in any form of binding or cover other than that in which it is published and without a similar condition including this condition being imposed on the subsequent purchaser.

The scanning, uploading and distribution via the internet or via any other means without the permission of the author/publisher is illegal and punishable by law. Please purchase only authorized electronic editions, and do not participate in or encourage electronic piracy of copyrighted materials. Your support of the poet's property rights is appreciated.

www.thenameofmycountry.com, www.oncewerecannibals.com
kiwipuss@aol.com

For

Dolores Kalom

San Francisco Street Artist and Dear Friend

Acknowledgements.

Bill and Susan Stepka, as always for their friendship and support.

The community of Street Artists at Justin Herman Plaza, San Francisco, California.

Edited by Linda Pedersen, 2016.

Table of Contents

Title	Page
Karanga	1
Burden	2
A Retrospective for Michael	3
The name of my country	4
White Roses	5
While my lover sleeps	6
Poetry in Motion	7
Spanish is spoken in The Mission	8
Raaga (for the performance troupe Dhaia Tribe)	9
A letter from home	10
Francisco	11
Broken gods	12
Afflatus	13
Portrait of the artist's lover	14
Someone's history	15
Smiling cannibal	16
Three simple words	17
Brother in Arms (for Carlos Nik Gonzales)	18
Read me carefully	20
Moana	21
Tama	22
Red hat	23
Jaime Cortez	24
An ode to the artist	25
Café Macondo	27
Woman in red	28
Rongo	32
Of ants and men	33
Glad to meet you	34
Call me when you're ready	35
Dolores	36
A stubborn child	37
Driving under the influence	38

Ask a young man a silly question	39
Michelangelo's little helper	40
Come rain or shine	41
Two edged sword	42
Photograph of New Zealand	43
Murmuration	44
The world before	44
Reunion at Café Brainwash on Folsom Street	45
Benefits of war	46
Taku kopapa	47
The fallen muse	48
Leaving for home	49
A poet without a poem	49
Fighting fire	50
Thank you for the green carnations	51
Our roots are connected	51
(untitled)	52
Speak the truth	53
Shopping in a brick and mortar	54
Echoes of home	55
A eulogy	56
Café Trieste	57
Love in a time of herpes	58
The chase	60
Tupuna	61
Wayward wind	62
The ego	63
Castle	64
The greatest love	65
Home is where the heart is	66
Read me your poems	67
Writing home	68
Sleeping beauty	69
Public spaces	70
Food for thought	71
Fog	72
Juan	73
Language of the dead	74
Shadow	75

Roots	76
Item 12 Roll Number 973152	77
Adios San Francisco	79
The pause between borders	83
Delta waves	85
The sound of water	86
Where the past is located	87
Back to the beginning	88

Karanga

The evening call of the karanga
Is a lilting note of waterfall
Pouring her sorrow on the emerald
Land of our dead.

There, in her dark voice
She is bleeding
Our young men have left her
To roam in a field of ghosts.

In the blue mountain
Is buried her echo
Forever seeking a barren river
To carry her sentence.

Karanga, karanga
You are a hostage in our land
A stranger among our living
A requiem floating in the mists.

To the depth of the earth you will return
Forbidden to see what our men have seen
Waiting for them to come back
To their beloved evening soil.

Burden

The fathers of poets are disappointed
At the reckless life they lead
Because there can only be one poet in the family
For there is only room for one failed life.

If the poet is true to his calling
He will fall victim to the excesses of life
Die painfully in a foreign country
And lay buried among the poor.

My father will not know I am a poet
Even if it is the one thing
I know to do with relative ease
And the last thing he wanted for me.

He wanted me to have a trade
In either carpentry or masonry
He wanted me to have more than he had
So people would not scorn me.

So he had me help him with odd jobs
After school and on weekends.
He spoke to friends in the industry
And enrolled me at a trade school.

My application came back
With the news he had been dreading
That I was rejected because
Of my penchant for the pen, not the hammer.

He took the news on his shoulder
And continues to do so in his frail years.
Still he mustn't find out I construct with letters
Lest our people blame him.

I would prefer to die
Alone in some distant land
So he can absolve the words I committed
And finally mourn the loss of a son.

A retrospective for Michael

Somewhere in the invisible realm of things
There are red and purple zebras with six legs
And large frond-like feathers.
They live in the silver lake
In groups of four and sometimes five.

They call themselves brother this and sister that
But all in all they get on pretty well.
Sometimes you can see them leap in the air
Or dancing some kind of waltz.

I go to the lake often, careful not to frighten them
After a while, the alpha male musters up
The courage to approach me
And then the others follow.

They have long eye lashes
And a smooth shiny forehead
Right up close I can smell them;
Hibiscus, gardenia and milkshake.

I hope to take you there one day
When you're not too busy or over-worked
When you make time for me
Or when I get the courage to say 'I love you.'

The name of my country

There is a tree with my name
Engraved in the grey bark.
I want to see how I'm doing.

I heard the property fell to disrepair
When grandma and grandpa died
And the others left our country.

I remember etching the sign of the crucifix
And watching the sap trickle to the ground.
I want to know how I'm doing.

If I make the long journey home
I'll search for the tree
Among the shrubs and wild bushes.

I also heard the other tree where cousin Pere
Hung himself was cut down.
They said Pere was a dreamer and a loner.

If I make the journey home
I will clean the fallen leaves and branches
And board up the wooden fence.

I will confront my name
In the shadow of my keeper
And accuse it for betraying me.

White Roses

I've been to the place where broken hearts go to escape
The rigors of everyday things.
I fell two stories and landed on a John Deere tractor
The place and the time reminded me of plantation work
When I was young, and the only thing that was important
To me was getting food in my stomach and escaping
The gauntlet rows of orange trees.
I had no understanding of repetition; the rows
Upon rows of bags, people and landscape
Seemed endless as the day was long.
I had no concept of time; the minutes seemed a crying infant
And the hour became an impatient child.
Adults were strangers and didn't complain
At the scorching sun or the menacing flies.
For some strange reason or another,
I ran over to the dusty tractor and drew an arrow
Piercing the heart on the dusty engine cover.

I've actually seen broken pieces of heart on the kitchen floor
In the prosperous country of America.
There was a satin ebony piano in the middle of the room
The furniture was covered and the drapes drawn.
The owners lived in the house a long time
But for now the house was empty and silent.
The mantel piece was lined with photos
And the hallway was swept of children's footsteps.
The bathroom was without the sound of gushing water
And the bed had two muted indentations.
The stairwell was not crowded with anxious people
While the television stared blankly at the family room
The creaks in the wooden floor could not be heard
While the cat door opened to a crusted plate.
The door swung open when I rang the bell
On delivering flowers to the lady of the house
Only to find bundles and bundles of white roses.

While my lover sleeps

The night is a mysterious woman
Scented and moist, supple and sensuous.
Her body; voluptuous and glistening at midnight
Crisp and tender in the full moon.

Her darkness is naked to the feel
Of sweaty palms caressing her black bosom
And groaning into her soul
Succulent and juicy at the crack of dawn.

Her ecstasy is the star
Shooting forth from her vast cavity
And casting the shadows of man and beast
Across the veil that holds back fleshy eyelids.

Oh, naked black woman
You seduce your man with secrecy
The arrow blindly penetrating its victim
Drunk in pleasure, lust and desire.

Black and beautiful is your name
Like music that soothes the pain
Black as the magic that liberates your spirit
When the prayer is heard in the shadow.

Your children dance to the rhythm
Of the rich leather drum
And make love in the darkest and most secret places
Of your sweet perfumed body.

Poetry in Motion

There is a poem in my belly
I can feel it like lemon custard pie
Waiting to paint a portrait
On a Sunday afternoon.

There is a poem in my hand
Jumping up and down
Youthful in experience
Ready to fly to the moon.

There is a poem on my lips
It is a cold glass of water
Able to quench my dream
Of yesterday when I was young.

There is a poem in my memory
As precious as a verse
With smiles that rhyme
Yet playful and crisp.

There is a poem from my past
That was never recited
Because the years were new
And the moment was innocent.

There is a poem in waiting
For you to succumb
Perchance to fall in love
For the duration of the poem.

Spanish is spoken in The Mission

Spanish is the language of poetry
Which I can't speak or understand
Especially the Spanish language
Forged under the sword.

The poet desires the red luster
Of blood to paint the setting sun
He needs sorrow from the masses
To complete his symphony.

A child born into poverty
Fuels the pen of the poet
And the displacement of her people
Gives the poet motivation.

Where the sword has fallen
Is the place to feel as one
Whom the poet searches out
To understand the metric beat of loss.

Spanish has to be translated
Before I can begin to understand
Neruda, Vallejo, Lorca or Borges
Otherwise it is just another Romantic Language.

Raaga (for the performance troupe Dhaia Tribe).

If I could speak the language of peace
In our time of war
I would count the falling tears of angels
Strung like opals
Contemplating
The silent breath of the incense dying.

If I could speak the language of love
In my hour of need
I would spread oil colours on a canvas
Green for yesterday
Candles of gold
And the echo of images in my heart.

A letter from home

A letter from an old friend back home
Made me realize the memories
I have of our past are scattered
Like tumbled grave stones.

Faces have decayed to oblivion
Limbs connected to different bodies
Smiles turned to gloom.
Now the sound of laughter is shrill.

The friend tells me who has died
In the long years I have been away.
Their images crumble to dust
And their breath causes me to suffocate.

She counts names
That sound strange in this country
And have become meaningless
In my book of names.

But there are certain arabesque names,
Amber cherub faces and impish smiles
That she fails to mention. It is they
Who keep the past alive in my heart.

Francisco

I searched for my soul today
But all I could find was bone
Hanging from the pastel Victorians
With intricate moldings along
The ledge of rounded ceilings.

My soul was there among the
Peacock feathers and lace curtains
In the silver gilded frames
Along the narrow corridors
And across the dusty hardwood floor.

My soul was reclining on the easy chair
In the middle of this fabled city
Of hanging hydrangeas and crawling ivies
Except the walls were friendly
And the people were lovely.

And there was my soul riding
On soft undulating hills
Pointing to Victorian ladies
And bustling gentle people
Where you took great delight.

And I heard my soul laugh
An audible skeleton murmur
When all I could feel were bones
And not painted Victorians
As refuge for my soul.

I searched for my soul when I lost
The stained glass window.
When you closed the door.
When the phone became silent
And I became all too Victorian.

There, lost among the splendid houses
And carefree among fairy-tale gardens
Memorial places to the roaming soul
My soul fell from the whispering clouds
And lost all sense of direction.

Hiding upon the thorny bougainvilleas
And praying to the white narcissus
I searched our vintage wooden home
For familiarity and consolation
Finding only the shadow of bones.

Broken gods

A wooden *tiki* stood in the window
Of a secondhand furniture store
On Valencia and Sixteenth Streets.
I asked what he was doing here
What was his *whakapapa*
And why did his people abandon him?

He doesn't answer, so I asked again
Kei te peheana koe?
And again he doesn't answer.
I study him carefully; the sound of the
Mallet following the chisel around his torso
The *kereru* singing on his shoulders.

He remained silent and motionless
A broken god among the discarded
And pre-owned furniture
Except the store owners do not
Know he is broken.
Two exiles staring at each other.

Afflatus

My body is decaying while I hold
This pen and press it against paper.
My weight is dead as I push
Down on heavy black lines
Deep as a hole in the ground.

I can't help but fall and stumble
Into the void and cold space
Between paper and earth
Where the words slither endlessly.

I only have one request
And that is for my public
To bury me completely in a mountain
Of compelling words when I die.

I want to enter the world of the
Dead poets, if it were possible
While I am still holding this pen
So I can describe that unknown country.

For now we will have to settle
For empty words and lifeless
Impulses, because I fear taking that
Plunge into the realm of poetic bliss
Lest I enjoy it and never come back.

Portrait of the artist's lover

A portrait of a young man
Looking up into the dusky lamp
The nineteen steps on the stairs
In front of him, closing the door.
His face is keenly ready
As the promising western sun.
It is the shadow of chiaroscuro
And the reflection of porcelain
Soft eyes speak of hopeful adventure
And destined arrival to a secluded corner.
A delicate smile overcomes him
It is in keeping with the composition
And livens the hour of evening
Radiating the moon and surrendering it
While the solemn purpose in his fiber
Reduces to a compromising halo.
Light does not vibrate like
Radical molecules of water
Guiding his mortal being
Towards a stranger
Experienced in the art of painting
Speckles of light on bodies of water.
The inquisitive traveler stands
At the solitary door
The aged wood framing his youth.

Someone's history

Should history judge a poet harshly
Because his life is filled with doom
Which is made manifest in his musing
Then let it be known that poetry is
Meant to free you from demons
That roam the blank pages and brick walls
 Holding back monsters and goblins.

His job is to make you fly in slow
Motion away from the dead corpse
Chasing you, while you kick away
Frantically, your feet inches from the
Decaying fingers. And you can't believe
That you're actually flying because
You know it is not possible yet you are flying.

That is the job of the poet. He will enter
Your dreams and orchestrate
Escape routes and flight plans to your
Mother's bed or your father's arms.
He will accompany you to your past
And be on the lookout for fanged creatures
Only to quickly whisk you back to safety.

He is there between the sheets
Observing your love making
He's listening to the slushy noises
The groaning, the stretching, contracting
Leaking, dripping, smearing and staining.
He's there cleaning up after the storm
Salvaging the weathered boards of home .

He is there when the child is born
To see the joy on the mother's face
The glint in the father's eyes

Is what has been described as
The river of life, the rising tide
The ripping out of the flesh
And the discharging of life.

History might judge the poet harshly
Because he dares to go where
No other man will go
To witness a flower blossoming into love
To bare the pain of rejection
To participate in dying; yours or a friend's
And return to recite it in public.

Smiling cannibal

Behold a smiling cannibal
Offers his seat to you.
He has the grace of a noble savage
The politeness of the jungle
And the courtesy of mud.

The light is foreign
Falling on cows and mosquitoes,
I rise from my seat,
You smile
And accept.

Three simple words

One day, scientists will pull
Love poems apart on sterile tables
And examine the little parts
That turn round and round
And the parts that go up and down.

They will discover love poems
Don't name you; only your essence
And the perfume on your naked body.
For now you shall remain nameless
Otherwise the poem will become a memorandum.

Formal letters ask for nominal things
Like the return of furniture or money
Whereas a poem asks for the invisible.
It asks all the gods in the world
To perform a miracle on the poet's behalf.

Scientists will discover poets don't know
How to honestly express their desires
Which is why they summon all the gods
And all the holy relics in the world
To help them confess three simple words.

Brother in Arms (For Carlos Nik Gonzales)

Wherefore our eyes met for the first time on a crowded street
When our minds focused on the details of landscapes and contours
Of our motherland, albeit our umbilical cords are connected
To different trees and wild rivers flowing in opposite directions
I know you.

At that moment, our eyes read the same writing
We know the road we've travelled and the fields we've plowed
On the steep slopes of the sun
Where the flies and birds drink our blood
I know you.

I know you from a police line
I know you from a photo album
I know you from a drug dealer
I know you from a cousin's boyfriend
I know you from a restaurant worker
I know you from a loving family
I know you from a gang fight
I know you from a church minister
I know you from a tag artist
I know you from a village choir
I know you from a school principal
I know you from a next door neighbor
I know you from a liquor store
I know you from a school dropout.

I know you from the womb of a spirit mother
The great whore who ruled the mighty waters
Who was raped by the kings of barbarians
And drank from her scarlet ocean of wine
I know you.

And of the angel that was cast from heaven
Only to serve foreign men in our motherland
Where we clean the blood from their homes
And the discarded waste from their lives
I know you.

I know you from America's Most Wanted
I know you from myths
I know you from Caesar Chavez Street
I know you from legends
I know you from Civic Center
I know you from soup lines
I know you from housing projects
I know you from travelling musicians
I know you from migrant workers
I know you from illegal aliens
I know you from exploitation
I know you from prophesy
I know you from my own condemned brother.

Wherefore we are reunited in this Diaspora
Of moving mountains and poisonous waters
Where our name is written in the sand
As destiny would have it to trample on
I know you.

While we regret our path's crossing
Like broken branches from an ancient tree
Let us conspire in the night the secret
Of our birth from the sword that conquered us
I know you.

I know your ancestral mother
I know your faith healer
I know your ancient astronomer
I know your ocean navigator
I know your wood carvers
I know your temple builders
I know your story tellers

I know your kings and queens
I know your brave warriors
I know your fishermen
I know your horticulturalists
I know your laughter
I know your destiny.

Read me carefully

This is the sum of my existence
This organic piece of paper
With the words I borrowed
From sorcerers and witches
Who guaranteed me
The words would come to life.

I told them if their spell didn't work
I would come and drag them
Out of their watery grave.
My bones are on this paper
So when you read it
You should feel a sharp point.

My feet are at the bottom
Of the paper so they can transport
You to the places I have seen.
If you hold the edges
My hands will grab you
And never let you go.

I admire the close attention
With which you study my body.
Hold me to your face
And breathe life into me
So I can go back to the sorcerer
And tell him his magic works.

A rare formulation of words
Is a colourless concoction
Capable of healing the river
And straightening angry mountains.
In precise dosages
It will adhere itself to paper.

Read between the lines
You will see the fortunate lives
Of other people I have
Wanted to emulate, especially
Those who practice magic
And who elude me to this day.

Moana

A young man asked the ocean
To give back all the money
He wasted on lovers.
He also asked the ocean
To give back all the time
He spent pursuing love.

It brings him a handful of polished shells
Which he places on the windowsill
The others he ties to a hanging string.
In the morning their shadows crawl
Onto his bed, touching his lips.
In the evening they chime him to sleep.

Tama

If I could empty the ocean of water
I would get on my knees with a bucket
And toil away night and day until it was empty
So that the sun wouldn't have a place to cool down
Or a flat horizon to hide behind
Instead the sun will always be a yellow beach ball.

If I could empty the ocean of water
I will find the shell that talks to Hawai'i
Or Samoa, even Tonga or Tuvalu
Then the canoe that you wear around your neck
Will fall off, and the octopus that clouds your eye
Will peel away like old scale.

Tama, don't let the ocean drown you
Don't let it suffocate your dream
You see, Tama, if the ocean were dry
It would be like The Mission or the Bay View
You know where the sharp reef is
Because of scavenging birds feeding on dead bodies.

Tama, don't get swept up by the under currents
Of the ocean but remain focused on the stars
To guide you. Tama, you did not sail this far
So you can abandon forty-five hundred years
Of ocean in your vein, salt on your breath
Or feeling the blue in your heart and soul.

But if the ocean is too much to bear
Then I wish I could empty it of water
So that the brown turtle on your back
Don't burden your stride to the liquor store
So that the flying fish don't get in the way
Of your gang banging and shooting and mugging.

If the ocean is weighing down on your conscience
Then I wish I could empty it of water
So the men in blue don't profile you
For being blue in The Mission or the Bay View
So the teacher don't treat you differently
Because you cause trouble at school.

Tama, if I could empty the ocean of water
You would lose your buoyancy and sink
Because your veins are blue like the Pacific
You would not be able to follow the stars
To a new day. Tama, you are borne of the ocean
And to deny it is to have no country in the world.

Red hat

It is time to pay my dues
To the homeless and the hungry
To the rooster and the fly
To mildew and stained cups
To tricks and lubricated condoms
And while at it, why not say
Thank you to art and poverty
To forty-three thousand English words
To inequality and injustice
All of them are life affirming.

If I had a hat I would tip it
To runny noses and silver earrings
To tight leather pants and the tomato
To whiskers and plastic chairs
To dolls and air-dried flowers
To mobile structures and eucalyptus leaves.

One day they will all speak to me
And explain why a boy stares intently
Why people sit in groups and others alone
Why Spanish sounds so San Franciscan
(Or should that be the other way around?)
And why the waitress does what she does.

I do know this; that when my tooth aches
I know the poor will always be poor
The hungry will always be hungry
The artist will always be an artist
They will never fade or go away
And the waitress will have new shoes tomorrow.

Come tomorrow, politicians will be voted out
The self righteous will be brought down
And the rich will lose everything
Contently, I share my room
With bottle caps and candlesticks
A blank piece of paper and empty thoughts.

Jaime Cortez

This is your land, it is not mine
From the pyramids of Uxmal to the feet of god
This river is your blood line, it is rich and sweet
From the golden mountain to the groin of god
This tree is bestowed to you, it is jade and azure
From the emerald valleys to the heavenly throne.

Where the jaguar roams from star to star
And the sun walks on red velvet walls
Where the rabbit kisses the face of the moon
And the serpent offers up a living testimony
Where the eagle paints a naked mural
And the rows of corn lining The Mission.

Your blood feeds the acres of agriculture
While your sperm nourishes the bay
Your skin holds together the mansions
While your sweat flavors the harvest
Your hair insulates against the long desert sun
While the soles of your feet dance in the dust.

This glorious city is yours, it is yours to give
From the urine flowing in the gutters
To the fortifications surrounding laughing houses
And the woman crossing the street with a shopping cart
One wheel missing, its empty housing spinning aimlessly.
The man shrouded in his waste has
Not the feathers to fly high above the tragedy
Of the forgotten and lost comrades waiting
For your god to pour forth his mercy
According to your stolen birthright.

Yet, here you are – a poor tenant in your own country
A poor immigrant among illegal immigrants
Paying with your sweat to sleep on your soil.
You're no longer the owner of your land
But a commoner among discontented commoners
And a peasant among endless peasants.

An ode to the artist

I can't write love poems like Joel, Jaime or Rebecca
I can't recite love poems like Rodney, Jamez or Marvin
I can't articulate love poems like Tommi, Michele or Moe
At any rate I think I know the mechanics of love
The general landscape and how they fit together
When to break stanzas and avoid hyperboles.

Janell says love is like the bull rushing towards the colour red
Jules compares love to an egret diving into delicious waters
Karen's love poems are predictable and on cue
Jerry's love poems fought in the Vietnam War
Lito found it at a SOMA night club
While Justin did it in a Chinese restaurant – ask him.

I don't know the words to use like Carla does
Or to arrange and deliver them like Blackberry can
Or Marci, or Brian, or Susan, or Michael, or Al or Ron
Nor can my love poems move the mountains
My love can't even break lose the chains
Or grow into a magnificent magnolia tree.

But I did touch an angel, when the poets were not looking
When the muse turned cold on the page
And cupid was momentarily distracted.
I touched an angel and tasted the ethereal magic
The poets speak about with palpitating breath
So precious and closely guarded by God.

Juba would have expressed that moment better
And Philip would have composed it with clarity
Timothy, Mark, Mary and Roel would have
Captured the moment without the use of cliché
But I was the thief that stole one kiss from an angel
When I touched him before the ink dried on paper.

When the poets were penning love on paper
An angel slipped away and stood at my doorway
While the poets searched for their inspiration
The angel escaped from their bed.
When the poets gathered for a reading at a café
I had kissed the very angel they were writing about.

Café Macondo

While waiting for an old man to die
I boil a pot of Earl Grey tea
Finding sinewy hair in the bowl of sugar.
He had brought a drugged out hustler
To his room last night, and for some
Strange reason the bathroom plumbing is blocked.
If he chooses to die with a hustler
On top of him then power to him.
I don't want to interfere with his dying
I wish he wouldn't upset my morning routine
But here I am going through the motions
Before heading for Café Macondo on Sixteenth Street.

Poets used to sing in this place
And dancers used to paint here
Dolphins, clowns and fat ladies
Are no longer at the Macondo.
Writing pageants and high school students
Elephant stories and copulating spiders
Fire eaters and water baths
Guns, papayas and runaway kids
Lavender, bamboo and oriental rugs
Robert, Lynn, a Russian Jew and a butch dyke
Yesterday's newspaper and an ashen kid in a black beret
Was how I remembered café Macondo.

I do my morning routine in Macondo's restroom
Only to find the poets of yesterday vividly present
I can feel their warmth on the oval seat
And their closeness in the dank room
They've left bitter verses on the wall and door
Some so deep the roaches use them to hide in.
"Be kind to the ozone: kill yuppies."
"Cut-and-paste is NOT art."

"End dot com gentrification."
"Death to the White ruling class."
I wouldn't be at Café Macondo
If I wasn't waiting for an old man to die.

Woman in red

Let the cold night come to me
Slip past the broad door keeper
Who is motioning a calm wave
In my trail of haste and foam.

I will return again tomorrow night
To wait for another red cap
To wildly step into these dark
Chambers, into the souls of lonely men.

Do not shut the lid of this
Establishment from letting me
Return for another round
Of comfort on my dry lips.

Here is the roll of a hard day's
Work to jingle melodically on
The wood and soothe
The heart of a gentle man.

Beat your bosom with
The hard of your fist
And bellow me a patriotic tune
While I wait for her over here.

From the same country as my father
Did she come in a red cap
And the magic of the Little People
She threw it in my eye.

Oh cruel, cruel is the black sky
Of our forsaken home
To smite me with her soft
Pale skin for the brief moment I held her.

Tomorrow, mark my solemn word
I'll not waste idling in circumspect
I'll accomplish it once and for all
If the devil be right and true.

Let me have her one more time
To be right she is pure and of our land
And I'll confidently go back to
My damp room a happy man.

For what is a man without heaven
Or a reason for a companion?
It matters only that she
Performs the patriotic duties expected of us.

A happy man is in the sight
Of conniving patrons
Who wager and quarrel
At the luck of like men.

I've not set foot on the sacred
Departed land of old
But my path is clearly intentioned
By many loyal men and women.

Their round smiling eyes
Will not diminish in the cold night.
Order me another round
And I'll start from the beginning.

Let me say unapologetically, Ireland
Is sad and waning in the past
There is a forboding stillness
On her disavowing people.

We should not expect other people's
Children to comfort our exile
So turn your fresh morning eyes
To me, oh lady in red.

Our country is weeping.
The sacred ambergris music
Lifting over the lichen stones
Of our dearly departed.

Let pity accompany us tonight
Make it a condition of our existence
So we need not explain it
To anyone, least of all each other.

Come holy green
And tall saints
Come nurse the glowing heart
Of our sovereign isle.

We sent red prayers
The length and breadth
Of the conquered world
To have mercy on the wretched.

Dear innocent lady
You are yet sweet in your years
Pardon the rash indulgences
Of the cutting night.

But I will hold back the darkness
The dangerous roaming lord
Of our mortal desires, if for a moment
And bathe myself in penance.

Oh, but for our blinding faith
We walk with sacks of piety
And scatter them to the afflicted
And the destitute of the world.

Woman liberate me
I am merely a man
An occasional visitor
In the depth of loneliness.

If you saw me in my youth
I was a shiny musket
Cocky as a waxing moon
And ravishing to the naked eye.

Let me have you tonight
We'll pardon the beguiling smiles
And tempest rumblings
Of these, I'll call my friends.

They are as urgent as the last of us
We have no one else to blame
But the crib of our mother
When she scarred us with her tears.

Come woman of the night
Come with the dark remedy of our life
You will help me hold the paved rocks
In my belly and wake me up slowly.

Yesterday we prayed for peace
And tomorrow we'll make the same requests
But I'm not asking too much of our people
All I ask is for you to comfort a lonely old man.

Don't fight the people of the dark
This is our refuge, this hole in the wall
Don't deprive us the moon
Even if our poets had no affinity for her.

Come daughter of Zedekiah
Refugee from the Promised Land
Seeking the isolation of our isles
Surely you understand my plight.

The surrogate land of earthly kings
We hid the child in the perennial rye
Until the dangers of the world passed
And left us empty handed.

Heal us woman with one act of kindness
You can heal centuries of injustices.
Give me what little is left of the night
In this dark room of wandering souls.

Rongo

I will come to you like a *pukeko*
In the middle of the night
Like a man bird a ghost bird to your place of sleep
And I will change into a love bird
A sweet singing bird, a fighting cock
When you dream, dream of a man
Dream of man bird, a ghost bird.

I will fly from *Ra'iatea* to *Uahine*
From *Moorea* to *Bora Bora*
On a pillow of dark cloud
When you dream of a man bird, a ghost bird
And I will ride on the crest of the ocean
And arrive to your *fale niau*.

The arch in the rainbow, *anuanua*
Will carry me along with soft petals of
The *pua* flower still moist and supple
For a thick bed to lay wide open
Your brown tattooed body
As brown as the scars on the *tapa* cloth.

When you dream of a man bird, a ghost bird
I'll come to you and make love to you
And when you dream of a man bird, a ghost bird, a woman bird
You desire my flight, my journey, my *mana*
When I enter, I will raise you
And you will fly like a wingless *tavake*
Beyond the far reaches of *Maina*
To the place of the setting sun.

There, I will clip off my wings
And mount them on you so you can fly back
Back to your bed of *pua* petals
Where you dream of a man bird, a ghost bird, a woman bird.

Of ants and men

I have two dollars and fifty cents and I feel rich
The only difference between me and an ant is $2.50
I am on top of the world and everything
Below looks like tiny little ants
The feel of copper between my fingers is invigorating.

When I die, I will probably be worth more than $2.50
The enterprising ants can devour my eye balls
And make dark residences of my empty skull
But for now, I have $2.50 and I am happy as an aardvark.

By the processes of reasoning and elimination
I believe my life to be monetarily unimportant
When all I can contribute to the well-being of mankind
Are unschooled words and undisciplined thoughts.

When the world cares less if I die today or tomorrow
Whether trampled on or brushed off the table
I want to write one more anecdote
Even if it serves to edify the least of us.

Glad to meet you

You will recognize the handshake of a lover
It feels confident and hopefully adolescent
He allows you to touch his naked heart
From the first shake you have rattled his saber
That is the handshake of a lover.

You are shaking the parted lips
That give slow pleasures
His eyes light up in the crowd
Steering you to a dangerous country.
That is the handshake of a lover.

He shakes the cage where you keep locked
Your petulant heart against falling
Foolishly head over heals
And losing your mind but you savor
The handshake of a lover.

As he pulls his hand away
He runs his finger across his brow
And then returns his hands to the side
Occasionally brushing his thighs
You have touched the hand of a lover.

Call me when you're ready

The barking from a dog announcing war
Is drowned by the speeding noise of traffic
Racing to a peace rally downtown.

Children of the post-industrial age
Trying to break the bottle that fed them
When the barking dog announces war.

They denounce their oil-hungry government
And the double-standard policies
It deploys on oil-producing countries.

Children of this generation have their hands
Stained with oil and are guilty
Of the crimes of their governments.

Enemies of their country will seek out
Those of them with blood
And oil on their hands.

The history of oil speaks of a people
Blessed with oil as their birthright
Which can be seen in their eyes.

They are cursed with having to protect
Their wealth from thieves and bandits
Who relentlessly steal from them.

The children of charlatans
Atone for their sins at peace rallies
When the barking dog announces war.

Dolores

Dolores said her mother (God bless her soul)
Made sandwiches (God help us)
And sold them to street vendors (God bless their hearts)
Without the required health permits.
And I believed Dolores because
She turned a stuffed piranah into a neck piece,
Snake bones into a choker
And a motherboard into an opera necklace.
Unbelievable.

One day a well-heeled lady with ample means,
Paid $80 cash, and Dolores only took cash.
She'll remind you the last time she cashed a check
Robert Kennedy got shot in L.A.
That, coming from a dyed-in-the-wool liberal.
So, she really didn't intend to connect the two incidents
But the lady paid with hard cash
For three dolls that Dolores
Strangled neck to neck to neck with a string.

Another office worker gave Dolores $100 cash
For absolutely nothing at all
But the lady said "you remind me of my mother in India."
Mind you, our Dolores is Jewish
And she's quite sure of that
So she pushed a free hub-cap necklace on her
But the empathetic lady wouldn't have it.
"Oh my, that's too bad, did you know that I ..."
"No madam, I didn't know that."

A family stood and stared at Dolores.
She told them to go buy a bottle of water.
The mother asked if she made her own stuff.
Dolores answered: "Of course I do, it's the law."
"How old are you?" the son asked but dad

Tried to block his mouth. "That's alright,
That's quite alright sir. Tell your son
That I am the same age as the Golden Gate Bridge."
"How do you know that?"

She turned 'nothing' into an amulet
And charged $2, the same price she charged in 1965
But if she came across a utensil, a gadget
A tool or an instrument, she charged more.
In heaven she's probably pushing a
Broken rolodex on God, or stiff bicycle bells to angels
Attached to a black cord for necklaces
Peddling her merry way since the day
Eve sold Adam a tainted product.

A stubborn child

The old people are anxious to hear word of me
And other children that have left without
Their blessing; they want to know who was right.

They want to know if their archaic ways can be applied
In the modern world and in my particular case they want
To know how far my stubbornness has taken me.

I want them to know that I am still seeing birds fly
The wind pulling up tall mountains and trees breathing,
And that I am living at the edge of the ocean.

They will not hear that they were right; I will
Regret the day I turned my back on them, that my soul
Is crying on the stern of a parentless wind.

It desires to rest in the refuge of familiar odors
It longs for the agitated voices of reprove
Only to recharge and set off on another adventure.

Who am I to deny the wisdom of their arboreal words?
They have known drifters from our country
Who returned home tortured from within.

They have also seen many sons discard their primitive skin
Vowing never to return to rustic identity
Seeking out another country wherein to be reborn.

Mine will be another story for them to caution
New generations of stubborn children
Who count the shimmering stars in the dark sky.

Driving under the influence

Amid the chaos of congested traffic
An old car, laden with bags
And other personal effects waited at the lights
In the middle of the many street lanes.

People from stationary buses looked
Out the window and pointed.
On top of the roof of the car was
A black coffin tied down with white rope.

It was not a funeral, so no one paid
Their respects, nor was it a practical joke.
It seemed the occupants were most likely
Pulling their roots and passing by.

It felt like an eternity, the mass of automobiles
Crawled but an inch, yet no one honked
The horn, out of curiosity perhaps
While counting down to the change of light.

Bike messengers maneuvered between
The lively bodies inside humming vessels
And past the wooden box atop the car
Seeming to travel on a parallel path.

There was no tragedy or reason to laugh
Time was in the box and nothing more.
There was no regrettable delay,
It was merely a practical reminder of life's journey.

Ask a young man a silly question

The creature posed the question to a young man:
"What animal walks on four legs
In the morning, two at the hour of noon
And three legs in the evening?"

The young man thought of himself
Making love like a dog, spread out
On knees and hands digging
Into the moist ground.

He then stood on his feet and
Wrapped her around him, lifting her
Off the ground towards the sky
Towards thunder and lightning.

Kneeling again, he raises his hands
And guides his mouth to the soft
Luxuriousness of a mature woman
His sweaty brow dripping on her.

But he decides to answer the creature
In riddle, so that humanity
Will speak highly of him
For many noble generations to come.

Michelangelo's little helper

My table lamp is a golden cherub
I bought at a garage sale.
He is standing on three elevated risers.
The first is lacquered bronze, the second
Marble and the third is cut glass.
Above his head is a round ball
From which is mounted a string of faceted crystals.
Above that he holds the large
Parchment neatly pleated in a circle.

He looks like he wants to relieve himself
On the night table.
He wants me to be still
And listen to his story.
He says he once held the robe of God
When the Devine reached out his hand
To give Adam the breath of life.
But when I doubt his story
I pull the cord and he gives me light.

Come rain or shine

I have resigned to poverty
Despite how much or little I have
Eventually it will all disappear.
Poverty will keep me company
Especially to that place where riches
Are not permitted.

If I make poverty my friend
I will not fade when I die.
It will lubricate the transition
Through the proverbial eye of the needle
I will walk naked
In readiness for that day.

Take me when I'm poor and beaten
Not at harvest time
Take me when I'm weak
Not when I'm strong
Take me when I'm crying
Not when I'm in love
Take me in the cold of night
Not on a sunny weekend
Take me when I'm guilty
Not when I'm innocent.

Tomorrow my fortunes may change
For better or for worse
So I'll keep poverty in my back pocket
For that rainy of rainy days.

Two edged sword

They will not receive me
Back in my home town
My words will sever
Any remaining ties I have
With the road and sky
Of that place in my heart.

The old people will deny
They taught me these words.
I will write them to say
"These are the words
I climbed on the bus with
When I bid you farewell."

How can I convince them
That it was a sword they
Gave me on the church pew.
I've used it in the kitchen
And defended my life
With it on the cold streets.

They will not like the way
I embellish phrases
Or where the words have been
During these long years.
But it is time I return them
To their earthly beginnings.

They have grown dull
When I spoke of compassion
And the words fell on deaf ears.
Our old people will find it
Difficult to understand
That we lack many verbs in our diction.

Let me return to my home
All I ask is a roof over my head

Just let me come home
The same way the others
Have returned in the past
And taken a vow of silence.

Photograph of New Zealand

Dear land of my people,
I saw you when you were a young man
Your vitality, I saw in an old photograph
I came across in an old book yesterday.
You were a gazelle with *pounamu* in your eyes
Venus had touched your face red
And the rain forest was in your heart
Gentle as the golden paddocks.
You were eager to run free
And cut the fresh earth with your feet.
At the river, you glanced at your beauty
Which you took for granted
And have no care for
Nor do you concern yourself with obstacles
Not even the consequences
Of being young and free.

Murmuration

We nurture the fragile warmth that has burned
In the heart of the revolutionary
The flame that fueled the passion for justice
And freedom, and the flame that inspired
The poet to pick up the pen and fight.

The flame that burns with hope, then dimly
Its life is tossed mercilessly by the wind
To the point of extinction
While we wait for the revolution
So let's pick up the pen and write.

We want to swim in the fire that tempered
The soul of the revolutionary
The flame that purified them
The flame that burned away the chaff
And made them pure gold.

The world before

The world before
Was a garden.
It grew wild with lavender
Over flowing with blue hyacinth
Perfuming the rows of rosemary
Garlands of red berries
Summer time yellows.
All of them marching naked
In the reflection of a slow river
Speaking softly
The creativity of God.

Reunion at Café Brainwash on Folsom Street

Before I decide to look for another creative outlet
Let me attempt another love poem, just one more time
Before the owner of this fine establishment runs his index finger
Across his neck, let there be one more attempt at a love poem.
Before the barista clears my table and hands me the bill
Let me try reasoning with all of you gathered here tonight.

There is no two-drink minimum, and no limit on love
You can love all you want, just remember to take some home
Tonight. There is no limit to love. It is as big as this room,
Comfortable as the chair you sit on, it remembers your curves
It fills your coffee cup and warms the tea pot.
Love is tipping the barista, and slipping him your number.

Thank you to this public hall, your helpful staff and host
Thank you to butterflies, gossamer trees and red roses
Thank you to dreams, for three wishes and email messages
To odd pairs of socks, to matching martini glasses
The touching under the table and that special look
From that special someone across the room.

If this were a church and my name was Cecil Williams
I would command all of you to turn to the person next to you
And to the person behind you and in front of you, and give them
A big hug, you see love is many things to many people.
I would command the destruction of barriers and
The laws that inhibit and confine us.

Love is a *venti* hot cocoa with whipped cream
It's an eighteen wheeler diesel powered truck
Love is a floral sculpture at Ixia's on Market Street
It's a fast photocopier at Kinko's at two in the morning
Love is a thick slice of pizza from Blondies
Love is a working spare tire.

Love is finding someone in a busy crowd
Like finding a valid Muni transfer in the gutter

Love is free and sometimes brief
Like free internet access at the library
Love is when you find yourself in someone else
Like looking at a clean seat on BART.

Love is when you hear the singing coming from the violin
And the wind from the flute flowing spontaneously
It is a thunderous roar from a group of tribesman
It is a yacht in the San Francisco Bay
It is a small airplane dragging a rectangular banner
Love is a request composed in a hurry.

Benefits of war

An army of medieval locusts waits to devour
The fallen bodies from our war.
They whet their mandibles
For the messy job ahead.

They don't discriminate between
The corpses of enemy and foe.
They are both eviscerated
The same meticulous way.

The desert will not turn cold
With the blood of our fallen.
Instead it will be carpeted with
Wild locusts devouring them.

When we have finished the latest
Of our wont for wars and taken account
Of our losses, the swarms of nature will have
Multiplied in readiness for another of our wars.

Taku kopapa
My body is a tropical island
Remote and isolated, removed and hidden
It is briny yet intoxicatingly sweet
Under the wavering Southern Cross
Crevices for pirates to bury their treasures
Natural harbours for sailors on Cinderella
Pointed hills to observe the heavens
An isthmus to plot the transitioning planets.
The texture is rough but smoothed by many hands
With etchings marking its growth
Its proportions and ratios are models for the *Tiki*
Not like that of Ganymede or Zeus in other lands.

Tane is the god of the forest adorning my mountain
Swaying to the reincarnating rhythm of a wooden drum
Big lips to bleed on the straw mat
And a nose adorned not by the Greeks or Romans.
Abalone eyes glazing in the thick night
And grey streaks bequeathed by the pounding reef
That guard the waves from violating my sanctuary
Allowing only the singing timid birds
To lay their plumes of knowledge on my mountain
My island draws sustenance from mother earth
And the man in the sky impregnates her with his mystery
When his longing tears fall for her.

My lagoon is deep and black for tall ships to enter
Flying the colours of red, white and blue
It changes with the lunar tides
Of new ideas, philosophies and gods
It subsides when condemned
By a new master or omnipotent god
It dies from foreign diseases
And its soul is ravaged by profiteers.
My body is the spirit of *Io, Ra* and *Pele*
Wrapped in a sun-baked carcass
My island is a gift from the gods
But my body is an offering to the gods.

The fallen muse

In the early hours of the morning I wait
For you to break through the window
And come rolling across the floor
Stretching your wings across my bed.
I wait for that spark to gently lift the scales
So I can lay my eyes on you.

My muse, you were not there
When snow fell in the summer time.
You were nowhere to be found
When lightning struck and leaves fell
From the mountain tops
So I did not behold you.

You lifted me from the ashes
And restored me from the trenches.
But when the mountain cried your name
You silently turned your face
And folded your wings
Leaving me stranded on the ground.

You have the effect of the butterfly
A memory of love birds
A sweeping eagle in the storm
And a yellow canary in the morning
A peacock at the prime of night
And a swan on a soft bed.

Yet I did not see you when the snow fell
In the summer of our life
Or when a streak of light broke a tree
Still I wait for you to enter through the window
And gently lift the scales again
So I can lay them on you.

Leaving for home

I want to invent death
And make it an open question.
It will be selfish and meaningful
Slow yet masterful.

I will ask it to leave behind an aching heart
To walk barefoot on the beach
Alone and weak, hoping
The wave will erase it.

I want to designate a planet
Where death can reside
Only to return when hearts are full
And the absence is long.

I want to invent the photograph
So death can dwell
For one generation
Before it can depart for home.

There will be a lonely double bed
A silent chair, an unread book
An empty coffee cup, a longing coat
And the memory of voices.

A poet without a poem

Should my family decide to trace
Their lost son, they will find me
In the tomb of the Unknown Poet.

I will be in the company of
Unpublished and ostracized poets
Waiting for someone to find us.

But as I write this I am afraid they
May show up unexpectedly
So I walk with one eye over my shoulder.

If they find me while I am still alive
All I have to show them are a faded collection
Of poems that do not belong in our land.

The collection will be of no worth to anyone
Because the unpublished poet
Is only worth his weight in gold when he is dead.

Fighting fire

This is the fire Desire stole from the heart
Of a young man from Nebraska
Who had the flame for a Japanese girl.
Desire dressed the fire in kimono and taught it
Basic conversational Japanese.

This is the fire Desire sold to a married man
Who picked her up on Polk Street
In a white station wagon at three in the morning
Where he drove to the Marina Greens
And made love on top of the child safety seat.

This is the twenty dollar bill Desire paid
A boy named Angel.
He said he was a musician from L.A.
And needed airfare money
But he stayed and gave the money back.

Thank you for the green carnations

I am going to paint you lying on the bed.
I'll paint you in the candle light.
Your shadow is stretched on the floral sheet,
The carnations you gave me adore your recline
They open their eyes in the clear vase.
I've hidden the imaginary sketches I made of you
Lying on my bed, but amazingly you're here
Posing for my brush and paper.

Relax now, let me dip the brush with your colour
A halo effect on the calming light.
Your outline is indefinable with shades of cream
And right there I need to dab the palette
To capture that most private part of you
So I flick and turn the brush, flicking and turning again
Your face reacting to the sabre strokes.
I gently blow the watercolours, so they won't run.

Our roots are connected

These words come to you from the pre-occupation
Of the descendant of a senile old man you
Fed kerosene and into whose cup of coffee you poured sand
When the old man came by your house to play
With your children and sing for lollies.

An old man punished by God and set to roam
The street begging for candy and cigarette
When he had his own supply at home with me
Waiting for him to return for lunch and
Off again to play with the children.

At night he returned with cuts on his arm
But he can't remember who hurt him.
As I cover him to sleep he asks if I've seen his
Grandson from many years ago when he carried
Him on his shoulders to the store to buy the boy candy.

These are the words from that crazy family with
The senile grandfather whom the preacher said
From the pulpit was possessed by the devil
And the words from his mouth are corrupt and heretic
So I don't expect you to understand what I'm saying.

These are the words of people
Who see the dead carry their
Coffee to the school yard
On top of pink elephants.

Tomorrow you will find their souls
Strewn across the cold cement
Soliciting for a one way ticket
To another time and country.

(untitled)

It has taken a river seven years of singing melodies
And the apple tree has shed many a fragrant tear
To replenish the calico valleys.

No more can there be the feel of awe
At the end of pointed finger tips
It too has dulled in the moving torrents of the river.

A valley grows tall and loud as the years
Multiply and scorch a line in our minds,
It was the beast that calmed the landscape.

These are the seven remnant years from that
Confluent meeting when the river ran wild
And fortresses grew from the desert floor.

Untamed flowers opened their arms and swam
Among the hills of summer
When occasionally a shower quenched the earth.

But that was yesterday and the valley
Was jagged like knives cutting into the mattress
Revealing many years fading in the distance.

In an instant your love turned water to stone
Where for seven years the river ran over
The jagged edges of that chance encounter.

Speak the truth

Of foolish men, I will say this
I have walked in your shoes
On that narrow and dull road
Covered in fallen debris.

The noises I made then
Were echoes of empty vessels
Sleeping on the dark streets
Like kicking an angry barrel.

The stories we tell are blind
With discarded scraps
The exculpatory lines
We hope will rot in the cold.

But, we fools will dig up
Useless pieces of conversation
From the myriads of potholes
Occupying the pitfalls of many.

Whereas the wise will
Pick at knowledge like
Fruit on the roof tops
And offer it with clean hands.

Shopping in a brick and mortar

I know who my people are
When I pay for a loaf of bread
With copper pennies
They don't dismiss me
Instead they try to sneak a customary smile
In the shopping bag without the boss knowing.

On days like this I seek my people out
I am not embarrassed to reveal to them
My poverty in a handful of pennies
Our poverty is an unspoken birth
We hide from others
The same way our forefathers did.

We were peasants two generations ago
We shared our days of fortune
Because we knew the day would come
When the god of harvest
Made a count of our deeds
To determine the season at hand.

Our roots are in the cultivated soil
And our hands are stained with anguish
From crying in our hungry years
Where the tepid nights of two generations
Have not cleaned our imprints on the fields
Until a copper hand unfolds itself to us.

It reminds us of the tight knot
Tied at the corner of the garment
When our people begged on the curbside
For copper pennies to buy pristine white flour
Two generations later we try to erase
The pained memories of the fields.

You recognized the agony of your people
In the palm of my trembling hand
Which is why I sought you out
Because I know you will not dismiss me
But you will try to sneak a customary smile
In my bag without the world knowing.

Echoes of home

In our land of no poets
How should our people
Acknowledge each other
In a new language?

Let us construct the aroma
Of poetry wafting between
Nestles of summer trees
To understand our home.

We will call it *po'ema*
For lack of history and clarity.
The man conspiring with our senses
We will call him a *po'eta*.

Let us teach him then
The language of the reluctant shores
And of the vacant skies
To conform us to the others.

When his angular words fall on
The perforated heart
Of our prophetic land
How should we respond?

Should we slide easily off his tongue
Or should we hold him accountable
For opening the candid sky
To the didactic beating of our shores?

A eulogy

You offered to show me the majesty
Of your country when you heard I was
Leaving after many years in your midst.

You said it would help ease the pain
And the mourning will subside
If you could show me the grandeur of America.

You drove me to the steps of Yosemite
And to the desert landscape of Arizona
To show me the Grand Canyon.

The highlight was when you took me
To the sacred town of Sedona
Where you ordered a glass of wine.

I said you were fortunate to have
This powerful nation to ponder
The creative powers that be.

A long time ago giants lived here
And carved Yosemite, Sedona
And the Grand Canyon.

They painted the canyon walls pink
Like the city of Jaipur in their
Grand tradition of hospitality.

Then the gods relocated the stone builders
Before the little people set foot
And marveled at their handiwork.

They took refuge here
In the rocky foothills
And extracted medicine.

But the healing has not begun.
Unintentionally, we exposed our aching hearts
To the natural wounds of this majestic country.

Café Trieste

Tony came by on New Year's day
Drunk out of his brain and happier
Than I'd ever seen him.

He didn't make any resolution
Except to say he wants
To wait out his death in New York.

He also announced that you told him
I was the worst lover
You had ever had in your life.

Yet I remember a blanket of roses

A glistening swan with diamond eyes
A eunuch pouring warm water.

I also remember Monet admiring
Through the swaying branches
And placing water lilies around us.

I remember Van Gogh and his chair
Making our bed from golden hay
And attaching stars to the blue ceiling.

Then there was the shirtless Gauguin
Choreographing our every move
In a circle of multicoloured mangoes.

I remember the Garden of Eden
The ripe delicious fruit
And the knowledge of sin.

I remember it like it was yesterday
But if you recall that night differently
Then I wish you a Happy New Year.

Love in a time of herpes

When there is talk of war
I lock myself in my room
And write love poems.

The last war was rather romantic.
A customer I had always ogled
Came to the café and broke down crying.

I guessed his boyfriend cheated on him
So I comforted him by holding his hands
Which were soft and delicate.

He was incoherent under the static noise
Of his transistor radio, which made me think
I needed to be more sensitive.

So I pulled him close to my chest
And patted him on the back.
The thick lining in his coat felt wonderful.

He grimaced and buried his face
Behind tightly clenched fists
But we didn't know each other's name.

"There, there" I said, running my hands on his head
"Everything's gonna be fine, there, there."
His calf like eyes glancing up and down.

"We started it, just now" he said "it's on the radio."
"I know we did, on the radio, there, there."
I began to rock him side to side, comforting him.

"Oh I feel horrible, just devastated."
"I know you do, there, there,
Don't worry, everybody loves you."

"Innocent people are going to die"
"Yes, yes, people, people, die, die."
I felt his hot breath down my neck.

"For the sake of some god damn oil."
"Yes, yes, oil, oil, there, there."
I closed my eyes and dreamt of paradise.

The chase

The people who chased the sun
To the ends of their long days
Brandished dry fragments of the planet
In their hands, throwing them high
Above the crests of the sea.

It is flat here; the furtive
Glimpses of evergreen and rocks
Embedded on their forehead.
What should they call this moment
Of unwavering desires in their soul?

Morning is a moment on the horizon
Two thoughts consider the pathways
Of planets moving away from each other
But the time will come when they
Will lower their arms in the sea.

Tupuna

Arise my ancestor
From the depth of your sleep
And walk with me.

Arise from the silent grave
From the soil of your labor
And walk with me.

Sing your war songs
And beat your drums
In the hearts of your children.

For I am alone
In this field where the *tavake*
Once walked on the land.

Arise my ancestor
And hold me in your arms
When the wind rustles
The broken parts of my soul.

Navigate my canoe
In the cold of night
When the stars refuse to shine
And the waves churn my name.

Awake in me your courage
To sail beyond the unknown
And to be fearless of the falling sky.

Arise my *tupuna*
And return with the sun and the moon,
Your round belly in front of me
And walking stick at my side

Your medicine bowl swirling
And war spear at my breast
Protecting me
While you tell me stories into the night,
And promise never to leave me.

Wayward wind

If I don't return to my people alive
I know the wind will carry my spirit
Back to them so they can prepare
My resting place alongside the others.

The reason for their mourning is evident
Seeing me there unexpectedly
But because I am there with the others
They will prepare me for the last time.

The wind will carry me nowhere else
To rest except to be with my people
Where familiar faces and songs
Will prepare the ground for me.

I would prefer to return now while
I can sing the songs of our country,
The happy tunes we know when we
Meet after a long absence.

Or the songs of discovery when we
Feel homesick or fall in love.
The songs they will sing when I arrive
Will be the cold searching wind of old.

Nor will they say all the things that need to be said
About me and about our people,
But these are the few options
I avail myself by waiting on this side.

I can feel the chill in my stomach
The biting in my bones
My mouth is stretched wide open
And I am blinded by the cold.

The ego

We shall have to explain
The bone protruding on our backs
When that final day comes
We will be asked the nature of our crime
To grow such an appendage.

"I abused two old men, sir
One was a perfect stranger
And the other a friend.
I hit one with the palm of my hand
And the other I frowned upon.

"Sir, it is not right that I am besmirched
With such a hideous growth.
I was right in my thinking
And stand without guilt
In front of my peers."

When they examine the spiny growth
To see that it is very black indeed
And the stench is overbearing
They will gather bushels of heather
And order me to speak their names.

Castle

An old man asks for the time,
The boy gives him direction to the bus.
The man chuckles, like he was a friend,
Asks God to bless him
And stumbles into the night.

Long alleyways and lonely
Door passages lead to the boy.
He is guarding the precious
Years of his distant home
A fortification we don't understand.

Speckles of light haunt the street;
Purple beckons the restless heart.
Some say the streets are unholy.
Souls lose their way here, where
A boy gives direction in the night.

The greatest love

Let me show you the wounds
In my hand and the cuts
On my head. There, on the floor
Is the pool of my wishes.

I do not know another devotion
That will make you aware
Of my servitude to you
But you can choose to come or go.

You can stop the suffering
If you will tell me the truth
Because I cannot be making
These sacrifices in vain.

Tell me that you …
So I know I'm not wasting my time
Let me have the truth in your heart
So I can retreat to the ends of the world.

Home is where the heart is

A poor man will find his wealth
If he searches for it in tiny holes
Digging and clawing with his fingers.
So too can a sick man find his strength
If he listens to a wise man.

An atheist will find God
As soon as he starts to realise
The miniscule wonders of nature,
The same way a leper will throw
Away his cane in the presence of a healer.

So too will a homeless man be able to find
His shelter if he builds with wood
And metal instead of cardboard
Likewise, a man will meet his end
If he tempts his own fate.

So why is a lonely man without a lover?
Why is he without a soul mate?
Why did God bargain with him
The most difficult adversary
A man must endure?

A lonely man looks out the window
Of his warm yet empty house
The fire dancing in the marble hearth,
The lamp glowing softly
On the chipped porcelain vase.

The candle inside the crystal bowl
Flickering the faint pulse
Fluttering the diamond moth on the wall.
Rows of books fill the walnut shelf.
The photos of friends inside the ornate frame.

Read me your poems

Listen,
Do you hear the rain falling in New Zealand?
If you hear the lilting of the burning hearth
Then you're listening to the poetry rolling upon
The morning hills of Ireland.

Listen,
More keenly than the beating in your shirt
Turn your favorite ear toward the young wind
To the water whistling on the wire.
It is the crisp sound of rain falling in New Zealand.

Listen,
Do you hear the bristling trees and trembling rivers
With stories to tell their young?
Their joy will ring true
On the soil they fall upon.

(Theirs might be the language of heaven
And the cold shrill of the banshee
But we are neither god nor cursed
Like the people of that land).

How I yearn to hear the rain falling in New Zealand
Travelling on small wisps of the wind
That I may be reminded of the new
And unabashed poems you write.

Writing home

My home was a white poem in the green valley
Where the purple octopus and the grey shark
Played cards under the yellow kerosene lamp.

My home was a pagan song near the medicine tree
Where the red rooster and the orange cat
Played with papa's new rope.

My home was a church sermon on the alluvial soil
Where the brown pig and the chestnut horse
Played the guitar under the breadfruit tree.

The prickly grass lived behind the cookhouse
And the gecko watched from the pool of water.

The sharp mosquito slept in the still water
And the cockroach flew from house to house.

The hairy spider waits for the fresh wind
And the land-crab digs through the floor.

My home was a mango tree and an outrigger canoe
It was mama's Sunday dress on a balmy day.
It was the banana tree when it rained
And the majestic avocado across the yard.

My homes are the stars and the moon
They are the moving images in the sky
Where the elephant and the giraffe eat
From a giant candy floss, as big as an umbrella.

My home is the face of an old man in the sky
It is the black dragon spewing fire
At the butterfly and the sugarcane
Just before night falls on the window.

My home is a castle I built
When I was young and my belly ached
And the tree was cut for firewood.

My home is where my heart and television are
It is where my brush and chair are
Where I play music with the octopus and shark.

To write home is to feed the pig and the horse
To play the guitar and chase the goat
And to live in the home I built when I was young.

Sleeping beauty

I feel safe when my cat is sleeping
It means he has taken care of everything
So there is no need for me to worry.

He is full and happy with his meal
The monsters will not come
He has made sure of that.

As a child I was afraid when
The big people went to sleep
It meant they weren't keeping watch.

So the ghosts could crawl past them
And stand over my bed
So I would hide under the blanket.

But when my cat sleeps, I feel safe
Because he has taken care of everything
And no harm will come of us.

Public spaces

When love comes to town
The red balloons break free
Floating towards the sky
Like laughter on a birthday cake.

When love comes to town
Red signs that say 'for rent'
Gleam from the windows of
Houses once forbidden to us.

When love comes to town
The eye in the peacock's tail
Winks at the dancing senorita
In her red taffeta dress made of icing.

When love comes to town
The polished castanets vibrate
In the hollow arch of her back
And her stare is a pebble of amber.

Where the matador awaits
Caped in regalia and poised
To pierce the heart
Of the suffering beast.

Where music of the arid hills
Plucked from celebratory instruments
Floats like falling petals
From a single red rose.

Where loving is no longer
A private affair, but a public display
Of two people's anguish
In a town they found in the dark.

Where the priests did not spare
The rich house or the unpainted one
Because they were no different
And lovers could rent them.

When he came to town she heard
The opulent sound of the guitar
The clanging of castanets
Stirred two people to dance.

When love returns to town
Our city will once again
Become a place for young lovers
To risk it all away.

Where the raging bull
Can run through the street
And a single red rose
Can bloom in the warm narrow alleys.

Food for thought

An old man is not starving himself
So he can know what it is like
To be a vagabond or a poet.

A poet is nourished by
Birds descending from heaven
With sterile food in their beak.

Whereas a vagabond
Is a pathetic individual
Without a hint of imagination.

A poet picks the pink salmon
From the trees in his backyard
The bread he buys from an ageless monk.

The poet will invite himself
To a table of thirteen men
Bidding farewell to a betrayed friend.

The poet can turn water to wine
Or quench his dying thirst
From the river sands of the desert.

He need not green his fingers
By counting oily coppers
Or meddle in practical matters.

A poet will die a quick death
Before the pangs of reality
Marry him to a vagabond.

Fog

I have the distinct fear I will return
To the arboreal island of my birth,
So I'll paint the colour of San Francisco's weather
Before embarking on the long journey home.
The easel erect, palette and brush at the ready
I'll begin with the landscape of The City by the Bay.

A young man comes to work in casual wear
His hair is dark against the sky
He will hesitate to light a cigarette
But apologizes profusely.
He likes to discover tucked-away restaurants
Dimly lit by outdoor lanterns
And enjoys red wine at home.
He is curious at the prospects of town
Though he can't help but be shy.

The grey deities in the sky
Folded their hands on the floral napkin
Then tossed gem stones
From their travelling pouches
To calculate in terms of lifetimes
And magical encounters
Of the wishful heart.

If I return to the warm island of my birth
I'll paint an ode to the mango
The adverbs of the avocado
The spirited adventures of the guava
And the sap dripping
From a newly severed tree.

Juan

There's the house that keeps my affection
Safe at night especially when it's raining.
My moment of weakness is inside.
From the outside it looks like a giant
Blue wedding cake plainly
Decorated without fancy swirls.

Inside the blue house that sits
Not on a hill or in a valley
But at the corner of Guerrero and Duboce,
Lives a boy by the name of Juan
Who recently moved from New York
To escape the roaring crowd.

The house is somewhat dull
Yet it feels alive when I walk by.
It has the presence of a twenty-seven
Year old Puerto Rican boy from New York
On a tentative exploration, away from
The crowded streets of New York City.

It looks at me from the façade:
The Spanish window watches my
Clumsy walk when I cross Duboce Street
Hoping to see his smile one more time
To satisfy my fading memory of him.
The style of the Moors lingers in my heart.

There's the house that keeps my affection
Safely locked inside, the keys thrown away.
It keeps the roaring crowd out
Where inside is a boy named Juan
Who showed me photos of his family
In New York and Puerto Rico.

At the intersection of Guerrero and Duboce
Is where my affection left me
And was taken inside the blue house
By a twenty-seven-year-old boy
Remaining locked there
While I pace outside an empty man.

Language of the dead

What is the distance between our two worlds
Between enlightenment and nuance?
What is the colour of the obstacle
Or the vibration of ages
Pulling apart the elements of our being?

In August you said your scribes;
Masters, all of them, were long dead
Buried in the choruses of the ascetic land.
What is it about the fertility of your soil
That I should step lightly on my ashes?

Why should they write our story
From that place so common to all?
If the finality of our poem
Is to apportion each equal measure and beat
Why then does the sanguine lark
Comprehend only the tonal dialect
Of your noble dead?

This much is known; once upon a time
A kindly race of people
Lived outside the gates of formality.
We shaped crude musical instruments
And crooned our own dissonant melodies.

Tell me then how did
Our common goals preclude
One of us for the other.
I will try in my desperate plea
To validate the orphans of history.

Shadow

There is no prison as lonely as the walls
Holding the heart of a man in solitude and anarchy,
No religion or doctrine more pernicious
Than the moat surrounding him
Holding his soul hostage.

He is a prisoner in his own dungeon
Strapped by stringy emotions
Torturing himself in the dark
And counting the days with his finger nails
On the wall of his mind.

He is the black spider that pulls
From the web of weary travelers
Who spend their fortune on the
Acquisition of wanton pleasure
Only to be devoured in their feeble attempt.

He is his own persecutor when
He commits unthinkable acts
Found to be guilty for transferring encrypted
Messages about his secret
Plan to rendezvous with you.

In there is a bottomless pit of anguish
To compose unrequited poems
Continuously brewing and searching,
It is waiting for you to set him free
From the clutches of rejection.

Roots

There are instructions in our genes
Responsible for the simple acts
Of stepping forward and falling back.
When they analyze the expressions
Of these insipid actions
It will be said these genes,
In repetitious combinations
Are the roots of earthly pleasures.

Item 12 Roll Number 973152

Today I was able to trace
Fourteen generations of my family.
I'm old enough to be a grandfather
So it is actually sixteen generations
Nearly four hundred years
Of exhaling and waiting for someone.

To see myself clearly I plotted
The names on a tree
That grew tall and broad.
It became crowded and heavy
With each additional generation.

The tree explains why we
Thought we were kings and queens.
It was because we brushed up
Against a royal crop of women, and
We trained to lean on each other.

It illustrates we did not encroach
The pious lands we stand accused of stealing.
Nor did we instigate the feuds
We harbor to this wretched day,
Turning us in our sleep.

How can I decipher the web
Of connections to find the
Reasons why I abandoned them all
Then flew off on a whim
To live in America for one generation?

In the year 1600 America was not a free land.
The indigenous population was
Systematically being exploited
Along with the slaves from Africa.
Could they have planted the seed for me to move there?

What is it then about the
Retractable nature of this particular colony
Out of so many captured lands
That a free man from Taravao named Parerata in 1775
May desire to put his roots in America but didn't?

During her Second War of Independence in 1812
Ena took Tuaraupo'o for his wife,
Sired three children in Aitutaki,
The eldest was Pere who married
Maria from Taha'a and moved to Raiatea.

In America's Civil War between brothers
Living in the North and South of the country
Over the emancipation of her slaves
Matae and Mere became husband and wife
And had eight children in Tahiti.

Or could it be that America's campaign
To liberate Europe in the early twentieth century
(At the birth of my grandparents)
That her compassionate act enlightened
The consciences of free people around the world?

I met a Japanese lady in San Francisco.
She believed in reincarnation.
Four hundred years ago she was a Native American boy
Foraging the plains of the Wild West
I told her I was Pocahontas, causing her to laugh.

Pocahontas was born Matoaka in 1595,
Five years before my recorded history
(Those five years are indefinable).
She was known by her people as Amonute
In England as Mrs. Rebecca Wolfe

But if we believe the Oriental philosophy of rebirth
Surely we can transcend the barriers

That bind us to one life and one country
Especially the boundaries imposed
By death on us mere mortals.

In the vast land of America that I emigrated to
They're trying to find ways to expand the
Words of their forefathers
Indelible in their minds and psyche:
To be liberated and free at last.

Adios San Francisco

It is not easy to say farewell
To a city built by the hands of dreamers
So ornate her golden parapets
The chime from her airy cathedrals
It is ordained, the melancholy tone
Of the beckoning milky wood.

Were our dreams sacred then?
Or were we young boys, abstinent
Full of purpose and wisdom?
Come with me to the meadow
Where my friend said
White egrets perched over the water.

It would not be common
For us to suggest the bed
We lie on is maligned
With many colourations
Of the truth we desperately
Seek and constantly seek.

Perhaps truth is too definitive
An answer to our dreams

Perhaps all we need is a taste
Of what could be.
But some of us will journey
To the dreamy land ahead.

Can I count on you to save
Me from the vulnarabilities
I gingerly bring with me?
Will you be my undying friend?
The clamor of the iron street
Is asking me sorrowful questions.

Those hills there are mounds of wishes
They tie with a string and send off
Floating like ottoman cushions.
Some will peel at the veneer
Of their young red hearts,
Others will fade in the sun.

Come with me to the cloud
Folding amourously over the city
Like delicate paper lanterns
And I will tell you the
Story of the ancient sailing *junk*
In a bowl of warm rice.

Who is that virtuous stranger
Standing in the cold silver water?
Let me tell you about the night
They poured red wine on the
Starlit streets of cobble and sand
One thousand years ago.

And where do they come from
The hungry and the rich?
Falling is an unwilling act
But some spread their amorous wings
In the yellow breeze
Blowing from the Marin Headlands.

But if we abandon the mortal words
To instruct the beating of our hearts
What mechanism should suffice
The art of practiced penmanship
By those dreamers of yesterday
Who bared their wistful souls?

On condition of anonymity
A lover is to be found
Briskly walking in the colourful markets,
And waiting at the end of the day
Tall stoic bridge constructions
Stretching from here to eternity.

You'll drink your coffee black
On the benches with Old Italian men.
They've seen everything, they will say
A man with a melodic voice
Impresses them these days
And perhaps a man protecting his heart too.

Hold out your open hand
To the wind coming off the Pacific:
She is the pearl lady of China.
Her suitor made outrageous promises.
They say a fat domesticated cat
Guarded the city's gold by night.

Come, give me your intoxicating hands
I'll place them on the carpenter's tools,
They are solid and kind.
Please help me say farewell
To the city that rose from
The hopeful ashes of many dreams.

If you also dream the youthful city
We childishly carry on our sleeve
You will understand the inadequacies

Of mortal words. But I remember the language
Spoken in the Stone Age of yesterday.
It predates the language of angels.

Could that explain the dormant
Affections we have for concrete shelters?
Regardless, can you accompany me
In my journey from this primitive condition
To the other responsibilities we must attend
In vistas we have not yet seen or tasted?

I saw an old man carrying a bag of bread
To feed seagulls at Pier Seven.
Birds from far away as Angel Island
And from the bright heavens suddenly appeared.
"Am I dreaming?" I asked the man.
"Yeah dude" he said "you're like in a real dream."

The pause between borders

It's been six weeks since I left San Francisco
(Um, that's a lame introduction, I'll try again).
Six weeks ago I abandoned my dream of San Francisco
(Too contrived, try again without emotion).
After living there for twenty-five years, I finally left San
Francisco.
(Rather bland though informative yet ego centric).
I left my heart in San Francisco.
(Cliché? Then how should I explain my affection for you?)

In San Francisco you held my hand,
It felt like the thing to do.
We walked on Leavenworth Street
Turned right onto Chestnut Street.
I pointed to the Art School.
You pulled me close to you
And whispered in my ear
Some of the school's many famous luminaries -
Jerry Garcia, Dorothea Lange and Karen Finley.
On Columbus Avenue was located a salon
Belonging to a friend of a friend of yours.
We mingled in the cool evening breeze
Of busy cafes and crowded restaurants.
You said Washington Bar & Grill
Was a favorite for you and your friends.
I tried reciting the love affair
Herb Caen penned for North Beach.
You'd heard it before and leaned your
Head on my shoulder
Arranging the lyrics in their right order.
In the valley of concoctions and merchants
Who relish the art of combining raw elements
Pressed olive oil and sweet black vinegar
Rises Coit Tower, the unassuming art deco
Atop the layered houses of Telegraph Hill.
And on the abandoned graves
Of Russian settlers looms the Joseph Eichler

Apartment building seemingly at odds
With the Victorian houses of town.
You said you attended the launching of a new book
In the penthouse of the Eichler building
And the view from there was surreal
And the city below seemed nearly romantic.
On the way home you asked me
Not to fall in love with you.

The heart is an ancient city
Surrounded by white stone walls
Leaning on the ageless sun
Where merchants from the mournful desert
Gather and grind spiced hues of
Red, orange and yellow potions.
They are timeless treasures to the Magi,
The interminable soothsayers of old.
Silk traders will call here in the cooling dawn
And leave with their caravans watered to the brim.
Fortune tellers live here sporadically
As do sages, scribes and tricksters alike.
In the octagonal courtyard are small vines
For incense and the occasional libation
But mainly the fruits are bled for medicine
Tended by perennial farmers.
Harvest time is a spirited season here
And the oasis is eternally flowing.
There are minarets and mystical
Men wearing the desert on their beleaguered faces.
Yet they will invoke a nomadic spell
They found in the tumbled grains of sand.
They will say God spoke to a simple man
Of the lonely and lamentable dunes
And instructed him to build
A marvelous city in His honour.

Delta Waves

We found a dominant sequence in
Our gene that induces negative emotions
On both pairs of the amygdale
In the temporal lobes of our brain.

It seems we are more inclined to feel pain
Than we are to experiencing love and peace
Perhaps due to our need to dominate
Dating back to our prehistoric hunter-gatherer past.

We created The Golden Rule
Only three thousand years ago
At the dawn of agriculture, writing
And the inevitable Axial Age
To temper our innate nature
And redirect the future of our species.

Compassion, it seems, is a byproduct
Of our imagination, not of our physiology.

Yet despite our nature to acquire food
And to breathe air by means of malice and aggression
And our history of inflicting harm
To kin and stranger alike,
Our conscious attempt to daring venture
Outside the urge of our natural state -
To the possibility of love and understanding in the world
Is a testament to our ability to imagine.

Those who dream in stages and cycles
And those who conquer our inner demons
Will say that these are vulnerable stages
When the heart slows down
To its lowest rate of beating
Near the point of expiring.

It is in that most desolate
And vulnerable moment,
When we let our defenses down
And surrender to the mysteries of the universe -
That's when we feel the pains of compassion.

The sound of water

My grandfather was born in Tahiti.
At the age of six he was adopted
By Harriet and brought to Aitutaki.
What songs, therefore, should he be singing?

Should they be the sonorous impulses
Of a forgotten soul?
Or should they be brooded
In the tyrannous muses of home?

Papa sang the foreign songs
Of the patriarchal land of his wife.
She bore him sacred hills and valleys -
Golden images on the shimmering sea.

For if a dispirited man can not
Summon the faint lyrics of his birth,
What ghostly melody
Should appease the darkness of time?

There's a land of memories
Beyond the ravages of time
Papa yearns to see again
But a young mother is all he can remember.

She is Tahiti, the forlorn lover
Running through the cold river,
Bare feet and broken,
Falling from grace to loving grace.

This is the sound of his motherland:
The calming water in his eyes
And stillness in his heart.
What melodies should he sing in his new country?

How should the guardian of countries
And the sentry of souls
Distinguish the alien sound
Of grandfather's abandoned heart?

He desires only to belong
To the earth of his precious children -
The little dancing ornaments of Tahiti
Clinging to his every word.

Tell me what you know about foreigners
And their strange behaviours.
Tell me what you know about
Exile and the fading sun.

And I will tell you the all-too-familiar
Story of fear and endless fear;
The bending of the will to breathe
And the cruelty of indifference.

Where the past is located

The memory is an instrument forged
In a hot furnace of red and yellow
Burning coal. Black ore is collected
From the pit of the earth's turbulent history.

It is an electrical charge
Turned on by negative and positive
Emotions deep in the cortex
Of the unwary mind.

Its function is to administer
The flow of stimuli to the center
Of a broken man's soul
And those of his dispersed children.

If he remembers the beginning of time
He will not enter the house
Of his widowed father
Or drink the bitter water there.

Back to the beginning

Where will I meet you?
Will it be at the end of summer
Or on the narrow bow
Plying The Ferryman's wake?
Will it be in the alehouses of London
Or on the trodden slopes of Galilee?

Where will I meet you?
In the buried veins of gold
Or on the wild horns of Africa?
Will it be in the heat of the moment
Or halfway between here
And the ruffled pages of heaven?

www.ingramcontent.com/pod-product-compliance
Lightning Source LLC
Chambersburg PA
CBHW032147040426
42449CB00005B/435